Reading Primer
R$_2$

Caleb Gattegno

Educational Solutions Worldwide Inc.

Educational Solutions Worldwide Inc.
2nd Floor 99 University Place, New York, N.Y. 10003-4555
www.EducationalSolutions.com

Table of Contents

Word Building Table 3

l i y						
y			w l ll		l 'll	
			y			
			th th			
			d dd	ed	'd	
e e			f f ff			
a u			n nn			
e o			m mm	'm		
e						
			s ss	's		
i e			s	's		
u o a			t tt	ed		
a			p pp			

1

f   f   d

ff   dd

'd

Table 3.1

fat	fan	fun	It	fit
fist	fuss	puff	stuff	of
mud	mad	dad	did	dud
and	end	sad	sadden	dust
sand	stand	mend	spend	send
tend	dent	ad	attend	add
	funny	daddy	stuffy	I'd

— end it, daddy   — tom is fit

— tennis is fun   — dad did it

— dad is fed up

— tim adds ten and ten

— dust and mud sadden mom

— dad is a sad man

— mud is not dust

— pat is sad and pam is mad

— sam's fit upset mom

— pam is at a stand

— if tommy spends it, daddy fusses

— did dad's assistant attend

— a fat man stuffs it in

— mom mends a tent as dad tends a stand

— pat stands up as tim sits up

— ten men attend a pump

— it's an ad on a stand

e

th   th

Table 3.2

6

the	this	that	than
then	them	path	math
thin	fifth	fifty	tenth

— this is a fist

— tom is fifth

— and that's that

— is it math

— that path is muddy

— this is not funny

— fifty yams in fifty fists

— it saddens them

— sam is fat and pam is thin

— pam is as thin as a pin

— it ends on this path

— on the fifth, sam is ten

— that's the thin end

— then sam sent pam in

— it is stuffy in the tent

— did daddy spend them

— dad is not a dependent man

— tom sat in the mud, sad and mad

— then, fifty men sent them in

— mom is independent, dad is not

— is it this that did it

— then ten of them sat in on it

ed   ed   ed

Table 3.3

dusted	mended	sanded	fitted
spotted	tended	tempted	stuffed
stamped	missed	messed	puffed
passed	stopped	summed	thinned

— I missed dad and mom

— pat dusted it

— a stuffed fist

— the pup stopped and sniffed

— sam and tim messed it up

— dad summed it up, that's it

— a spotted mat is in the tent

— I spotted it on this path

— tim mended the pants

— pam sanded the steps

— I stopped the mad man

— pat and pam sunned on the sand

— pat stamped and stamped and stamped

— mom and dad tended the stand

— the thin man tempted them

— sam dumped sand on tom

— pam passed us and sat on the steps

— as fast as mom mopped it, tom messed it up

— I puffed it and puffed it and it puffed

— it fit sam's span

— pat dusted the sand dumped on the mat

a   u   i

                      y

           | w

           ‖
_____
           |

         ’‖

Table 3.4

14

let	tell	less	sell	lad
pal	lap	lit	till	land
lot	last	plus	ill	self
fell	pill	fill	sill	still

lass   slept   sunset

smell   smelled   spill   spilled

wit   will   with   wet   well

went   swim   swell   was

my   mind   find   wild   I'll

until   unless   upon   unwell   unwind

wind   wind

— I slept well

— did dad sell it

— let's add fifty and fifty

— will pat find the pills

— was it the wind that did it

— wind it up in the wind

— tell us if it smells

— I'll stand still on the sill of the mill

— my dad swam until sunset

— a wild lad spilled mom's pills

— did dad mind that tom went with sam

— it went well until tim slept on pat's lap

— dad lent less and less

— with this and that, same was not in at sunset

— the sun set as tom tilled the land

Word Building Table 4

o				ng			
l i y							
oo u				g gg			
y e				h b bb			
y				r rr re		re	
o oo	wo			w k ke ck			
				l ll	l le 'll		
				y			
				th			
u e o				d th dd de ed	'd		
e o				v f ve	've		
a u i				f ff			
o				n nn ne			
e a				m mm me	'm		
ee				s ss se 's			
i e				s ss 's z			
u o a				t tt ed d		't	
a				p pp pe			

	a		u			
			o			
			e			

me	ne	ve	d	le	k	r
	've				ck	re
					ke	re

Table 4.1

rat   ran   run   red   rest

rust   fire   wire   kit   kid

kill   kiss   milk   silk   skip

skill   sick   ask   sister   track

truck   struck   strike   strip

fine   mine   line

kind   after   dime

time   pile   mile

any   many   love   loved   lovely

fur   word   world   work   were

like   liked   live   live

dress   undress   dresser   address

— I've not done it yet

— the rat ran a mile

— sister, kiss my doll

— I did not mind it

— the truck struck a wire in front of my tent

— did tim find it in time

— the miners went on strike

— were any of the furs that pam likes in that tent

— ask sam if the strike is still on

— is that lovely dress mine

— five skilled men were at work in the mine

ee   i   e

o

ss   de   rr   b   h   g

se   bb   gg

Table 4.2

hat   has   hit   his   him

her   hot   hurt   hunt   hill

hide   hidden   hundred

bad   bed   back   black   brick

but   by   burn   been   brother

ribbon   worry   sorry

there   possible   impossible   promise

get   got   give   given   hug

leg   beg   egg   grin   big

bigger   beggar   lesson   possess

— sam hid it in his hat

— sorry, I struck at it but I missed

— my little brother is impossible

— a hunt went up on the hill

— the egg was burned in the pan

— the beggar begged with a big grin

— it has been hot and meg's leg hurts

— pat and tom worry a lot

— tell her that the ribbon is not on the pup's neck

— it was given in the lesson, but sam did not
understand it

— bricks get black but will not burn

— my big brother and little sister worry mom,
but I still love them a lot

— give her the bigger egg and give tom a little
hen

o   U   o

  oo   oo

wo

z   pe   't   v   ng

Table 4.3

26

do   pool   tooth   fool   stool

move   to   too   two   zoo   zip

put   pull   full   foot

hook   book   took   look

go   no   old   told   zone

gold   hope   don't   won't

very   never   ever   sing   zest

ring   hung   moving   giving

putting   from   lion   among

— don't worry   — there it is

— I'm sorry   — I won't look

— move a little

— don't put it there

— give five to him and five to her

— my little brother is only two

— the haves and the have-nots

— I too had to give him two

— little by little the fat man got bigger

— at the zoo tim was bitten by a rat

— I love that old brick oven

— is it possible that mother has apples in her basket

— pat is giving some bottles to tom and putting the rest in a pile

— do it with zest

— letters go faster if I zip them

— lions do live in zoos

— the zipper on my trunk broke

— there is nothing to do

— don't bother him with this

— I'm letting the dentist pull my tooth

— don't bet on it

— I'm sorry, I took the book and did not put it back

— mom and dad promised us a trip to the zoo

— did I give sam her address

— it is not good to give food to most animals at the zoo

— the family has not moved yet

— her big brother is a worry to her family

— if I give her this work, I'll have to find her an assistant

— I'm independent most of the time

mom and dad promised us a trip to the zoo. seven of us will go: pat, pam, sam, tom, mom, dad, and myself. pat and pam like the lions and tigers best. tom and sam prefer the wild birds. I hope to ride a pony.

it will be my first time at a zoo. I've looked at many books on animals and mom has told me other things. I'm having fun planning the trip.

my brother tom is fond of dad and I'm fond of mom. if we go on a trip I stick with mom, and tom with dad. we are happy like that, and mom and dad are too.

but sometimes it is fun to swap and I go hand in hand with my dad, and my brother with mom. both parents like us to do this.

Word Building Table 5

ou	hou	ow			o
u					
o	oe	ow	oa		
a	ay	ey			
l	i	y			
o	a				
oo	ou	u			
a	ai	e			
e	ee	ea	y	i	eo
o	oo	ou		wo	
a					
o	a				
u	e	o	i		
e	o	ou			
a	u	i	io	ie	
o	a				
e	a				
i	y	ee	e		
u	o	a	oo	oe	
a					

x						
qu						
j	g	d	dge	ge	dg	dj
ng	n					
ch	tch	t				
sh	ch	t				
g	gg	gu				
h	wh					
b	bb	be				
r	rr	re		r	re	're
k	ke	ck	c	ch	lk	
w	wh	l	ll	le	'll	
		l	le	'll		
y						
th						
th	the					
d	dd	de	ed	ld	'd	
v	f	ve	've			
f	ff	fe	lf			
n	nn	ne				
m	mm	me	'm			
s	z	ge				
s	ss	se	's	c	ce	
s	ss	se	's	z		
t	tt	te	ed	d	't	
p	pp	pe				

e   o   a   u

ee

te   se   le

'll

Table 5.1

he   be   we   the   me

these   see   seen   keep   feet

date   hate   late   mate   male

take   make   made   fatal   female

same   lame   tame   name   state

or   for   nor   more

horse   morse   worse

bone   home   nose   woke   pope

pipe   spoke   broke   broken   smoke

use   usual   refuse   united

rose   hose   woken

she'll   he'll   we'll

— we woke up late.

— these united states...

— he bets on horses.

— I've broken my promise.

— to be or not to be...

— I had a late date.

— mom woke me from a deep sleep.

— we've got the same name.

— take them home and feed them well.

— sam is on horseback with his brother.

— the bone in my nose is broken.

— the males spoke more than the females.

— men promise not to smoke but do not keep that promise.

— this man is the worst morse coder she'll ever meet.

i   o

c   're   fe

lf

Table 5.2

girl   first   firm   fir   burn

skirt   hurts   nurse   purse   bursts

cut   cute   cat   cab   can

can't   cast   cabin   we're

log   bog   fog   off   dog

song   gone   brag   bring

able   mable   table   capable

come   came   some   cover

life   safe   calf   half

— there was mold on the food.

— the nurse has tape in her purse.

— her broken leg is in a cast.

— I told her to be bold. I can't do it for her.

— don't tell her no, pam can't take it.

— he broke twelve eggs in a little pan. it was a big mess.

— the cut on his leg hurt him badly.

— there's no fire in the log cabin so it gets cold.

— you can find old beggars here and there.

— the cute little mice made that cat mad.

— I can't find a cab.

— the tire burst. we can't drive to the store.

— we're not that old, only fifty.

— sing a song that will make them weep.

— skirts had wires to hold them wide open.

— don't cast the dice unless I ring the bell

— I can see the end of the tunnel.

— is there no good use of refuse.

— we'll refuse to use homemade food if we can
  find similar products made by capable firms.

— fifty states were united to form the
  united states: thirteen in 1776 and the
  others, one by one, till 1959.

— I'll let pam go home alone if there is a safe
  cab to take her there.

— he has three girls. two of them became
  doctors.

— the first came begging and we told him to
  go. the second came too but he did not go
  as we told him to.

— some prefer to be told: do this or do that.
  others prefer to be given a task and told
  nothing.

sam liked homemade food better than
that sold in stores. he got the ingredients he
needed, prepared them, and cooked them on
his stove. some food needed a lot of time on
the flame before it became soft. others cooked
in no time, and sam liked these best.

sometimes sam ate his food cold, but if he
had the time, he put it on the stove and let it
get hot before taking it to the table.

if sam had visitors, he gave them the
same food he ate. his visitors loved it and were
happy.

oe   oe   ou

oo

                be   n

Table 5.3

42

goes   toes   globe   robe   open

does   done   month   months

ink   think   sink   thank   bank

both   bankrupt   hungry   hand

dirty   hundred   thirty

golden   thirsty   before

singer   finger   difficult

very   every   even   over

drink   drank   drunk   alone

you   youth   youths

blood   flood

— thanks a lot.

— if I'm gone for months, will you miss me?

— come, come, it's not so difficult to stop bad habits.

— I drank a very cold drink and it hurt me.

— he spilled red ink on the black robe and made it look dirty.

— even if you ask me, I won't come.

— at the bank he was told that sam is bankrupt.

— tim, will you give me a hand?

— not every person can sing as well as the singer we met at pam's.

— if it goes well, we'll come together and even bring the dog with us.

— he poked his finger in a hole full of crabs and got bitten.

— thirty-three thirsty, hungry men came along and were given food and drink.

i

ce	ch	sh	ch
		ch	tch
			t

Table 5.4

shop   ship   shut   shock   she

shred   shrill   wish   shell   shall

short   shot   shy   ash   push

chef   chicago   machine   police

such   much   child   chest   children

chicken   church   chin   china   chinese

witch   pitch   match   batch   clutch

lace   place   race

vulture   adventure   nature

chorus   manufacturer   orchestra

chrome   school   characters

— sam goes home after lunch.

— the old man told the children lovely stories.

— three men will box in two matches.

— shy men don't push.

— chinese is spoken in the churches of china.

— cooking potatoes in hot ashes was the chef's idea.

— in that place, the orchestra and the chorus work together.

— the batch of papers was sent to the shredding machine.

— she had a shock as the children in her shop broke some bottles.

— he pulled, she pushed, and finally got it in the room.

— she did not wish it to be seen, so she tore it into shreds.

— nature's adventures match those of manufacturers

a   a   ea   a

ai

the

Table 5.5

are   car   far   arm   farm

charm   father   farther

air   hair   pair   fair   chair

care   dare   fare

bare   pare   share

easy   easier   clean   eat   tea

meat   team   each   teach   reach

cheap   real   beach

peach   preach   breathe

want   wash   watch   wasp

— chicago sells machines to the world.

— in that shop you can find good things that sell cheaply.

— we no longer go barefoot.

— he is part of the school chorus.

— do you like fish and chips?

— the witch in the story was ugly and bad.

— this car will race in the indianapolis five hundred.

— my child likes children, and children like him.

— did you watch the tennis match on channel two?

— michigan is the state of car manufacturers like ford.

— china is much more populated than the united states of america, but it's surface area is not much bigger.

— clean air is better than fresh air.

— I don't care if the fare is a hundred. I still must go.

the children asked dad to tell them a story. he sat on the carpet with his children in front of him. he asked them, "do you wish me to tell you a fairy tale or something from my life as a child?"

the children responded, "yes, yes, tell us something of you as a child, not a fairy tale."

and dad started. "I was born in the chicago area, north of the city and near the lake. at that time the lake was clean and my two brothers and I swam in it every summer.

the children interrupted, "no, no, tell us something else, something funny."

but dad became silent and did not find a story to tell them.

during the month of april we like to hike and use the bikes. in this area there is mostly flat land and some smooth slopes, so it's not difficult to ride. and with ten speed bikes, we can go on and an until we're really tired.

if we stop to drink, we also think of having a bite. the food we take with us is good. after riding for some time, we stop and sit on the grass. we take the basket off the back of the bike rack, sink a hand in it, and find the things we need at that moment.

we love this kind of life!

io	y	s	t	j	x
ou		z		d	
ie		ge		g	
				ge	
				dj	
				dge	
				dg	

Table 5.6

job   jog   josh   jack   jet

soldier   just   schedule

gem   gym   germ   giant   general

myth   mystery

age   cage   george

adjective   judge   judgment

vision   azure   garage

box   ax   ox   oxen   taxi   axle

text   context   pretext   next

education   taxes   generation

spontaneous   gadget   gorgeous

— every morning josh jogs for an hour in the park.

— the next time jack comes home, he will no longer be a soldier.

— george is a giant, six foot ten and a bit.

— you'll find more words on the next pages.

— "make up your mind," said the judge.

— in a general's judgment, soldiers' schedules are all important.

— his job is to find the best adjectives.

— at his age, he is spontaneous but still wise.

— jack was paged as he parked his car in the public garage.

— from the context, he imagined that she was gorgeous.

— germs make us sick, gems happy.

— the jet age started a few years before nineteen sixty.

— I needed a taxi to take me home, but none would stop to pick me up.

a   eo   a   ou   ay

ey

ld   lk   gu   qu

Table 5.7

60

all   call   fall   ball   hall

small   false   water   walk   talk

guard   guardian   guess   guest

guy   guarantee   guild   guide

war   warm   warn

quick   quite   quickly

quietly   quiet   question

quarrel   quest   quiz   quarry

quo   quintessence   quid

walking   falling   people

wood   would   could   should

day   way   always   play   they

— I questioned her quietly.

— everybody can walk fast, but not everybody can talk fast.

— to be understood, talk must be neither too slow nor too fast.

— the quiz was not quite finished, but he left just the same.

— that guy quarrels with anybody anytime.

— in a quid-pro-quo manner, he got something every time he gave something.

— status quo tells that things have not changed.

— did peter only give water to his guests?

— can you guess my mother's name?

— in the talk show, there was a lot of small talk.

— by falling back on his first position, he guaranteed his success.

— quarry workers joined a guild.

— the hall was cold. she wished she had her quilt with her.

oa   ou   o

ow   hou

            ow

wh   r   wh   c

Table 5.8

joan   loan   loaf   loaves   soap

boat   coat   coast   roast

throat   tomorrow   fellow   follow

out   our   hour   found   house

now   how   frown

one   once

what   when   why   which

where   whether   while

white   wheel   whisper

who   whose   whom

circus   circle   recent   cent

— joan put on her coat as she got into the boat.

— he found out at once that it was not for him.

— when can you be with me?

— how can you do all that in one hour?

— do you suspect who did it?

— that man in white whispers all the time. he's tiresome.

— why can't you tell the truth?

— he told the king, "whatever you wish, sir, will be done."

— in that family, roast lamb is eaten every week.

— "follow that fellow", said the boss.

— what do you think of the mess joan is in?

— whose house is this? I want to visit it tomorrow.

— the same brands of soap and the same loaves are found everywhere from coast to coast.

— you have a call.

— he's such a small fellow, but so strong.

— my vision is very good, twenty-twenty.

— ox carts are still used for transportation in india.

— follow those fellows until tomorrow.

— since nobody told me anything, I found nothing.

— the judge left his large, azure car next to the green garage.

— please bring me a ball from the closet down the hall.

— in the northeast of the united states, the colors of the leaves on the trees during the fall are simply gorgeous.

— it is quite an adventure to go out by oneself in some places.

— at one time, there were a few juke boxes playing very loud music in every public place.

— young people nowadays watch t.v. for many hours a day but may suddenly find it boring

— there are so many books to read that you can always find a few that you like.

the judge sat in judgment of the criminal. the jury had found him guilty on all counts. he had stolen gems from the jewelry shop, hoping to sell them at once so no one would find the evidence on him. as a guard tried to stop him, he pushed the guard onto the floor. he jumped in his car and started to drive away. he lost control of the car and hit a police car. the officers chased after him and told him to stop. he didn't listen and rammed into another car and into a shop before he was arrested.

so the judge sent the criminal to prison for many crimes. the gems were returned to the store and it was lucky that the police officers were not hurt in the crash. perhaps he will come out of prison wiser and less violent.

I'll tell you a story. once upon a time there was a fairy who liked to visit children and give them gifts which are useful. once she chose to visit a house where a large family lived. in that house, there were seven children who ranged in age from three to eleven. the fairy wanted to give each one what he or she needed.

to the little one she gave a box full of cars of all colors and makes. to the oldest she gave a crate of comic books. to the three girls in between she gave a bike, roller skates and a scooter. she also gave helmets and elbow guards which were arranged by size.

to one of the boys in between she gave a chemistry set to do experiments with. to the other she gave a soccer ball with a net so all the children could play with one another.

each of the children was pleased since

the fairy had guessed precisely what each had
wished for. for twelve months the seven
children spent many hours with the toys.
the fairy came to visit the children often. she
was able to see them, but she was invisible to
them.

shapes can be regular. some of them are called triangles, circles, rectangles. they are also called geometrical figures. if you look around, you will see how widely these shapes are used. the tiles on the floors of your kitchen and your bathroom, the windows, the glass panes in them, the furniture, all show that carpenters and architects use geometry when making houses or furniture.

look around once more and find where circles have been used.

can we imagine how our ancestors used to live in the past, without running water, bathrooms, and other conveniences? homes had fires and could be kept warm. but when it was hot, it was only possible to open windows and doors or use hand fans. there were no electric fans or other cooling systems.

there are lots of places all over the world still like that. but we get used to progress and think that what we have now must have been around at all times.

this, of course, is not a fact. but we don't miss what has not yet been invented.

the baby was in the pool
could she be swimming
at only sixteen months
she loved it all
as if it had been her world
forever
but it was her first time
and I looked with amazement
where had she possibly found out
how to float
how to be comfortable in the water
how to keep from swallowing
and being choked
when she put her face
down in it
there she was
happy and quiet
letting the water lift her up
and looking up with a smile